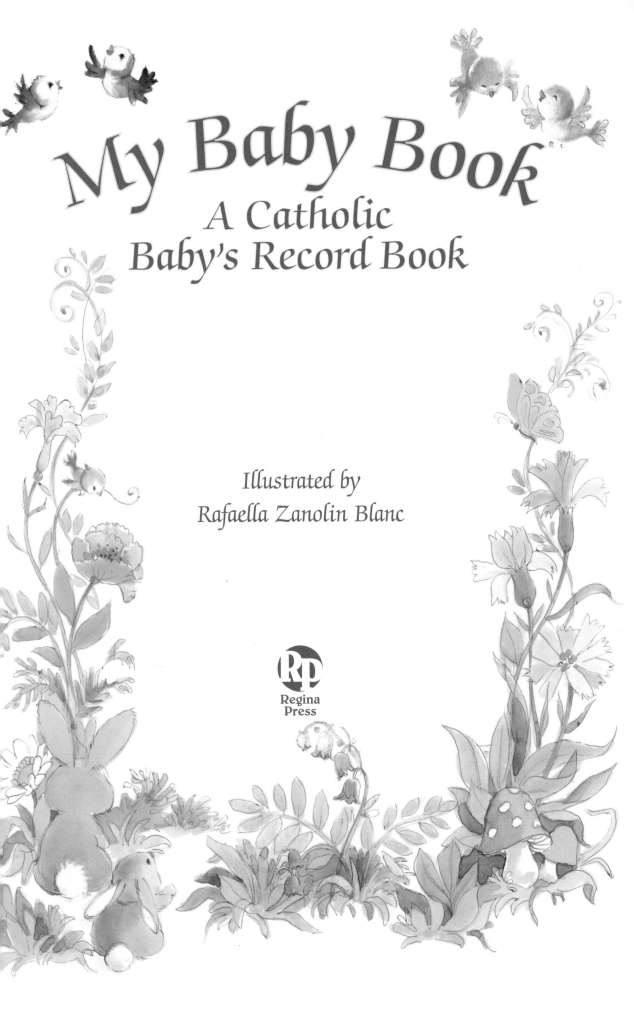

My Baby Book
A Catholic Baby's Record Book

Illustrated by
Rafaella Zanolin Blanc

Regina
Press

THE REGINA PRESS
10 Hub Drive
Melville, New York 11747
www.reginapress.com

ISBN: 9780882715575

Printed in Hong Kong.

Table of Contents

My Birth Certificate

And Jesus called to them, saying "Let the little children come to me, and do not hinder them, for to such belongs the kingdom of God."

Luke 18:16

My Birth

My name is _____

I was born at _____ o'clock _____ M

on _____ Date

at _____ Place

in _____ City, State

Doctor _____

Pediatrician _____

Nurses _____

I weighed _____ lbs. _____ ozs.

and measured _____ inches _____

My hair was _____ and my eyes were _____

I was named _____

because _____

_____

I was the _____ child

of (Father) _____

and of (Mother) _____

My home was at _____

_____

_____

11

My First Photograph

"And a little child shall lead them."

Isaiah 11:16

Visitors and Gifts

Name   Gift

_____   _____

_____   _____

_____   _____

_____   _____

_____   _____

_____   _____

_____   _____

_____   _____

_____   _____

_____   _____

_____   _____

_____   _____

My Family Tree

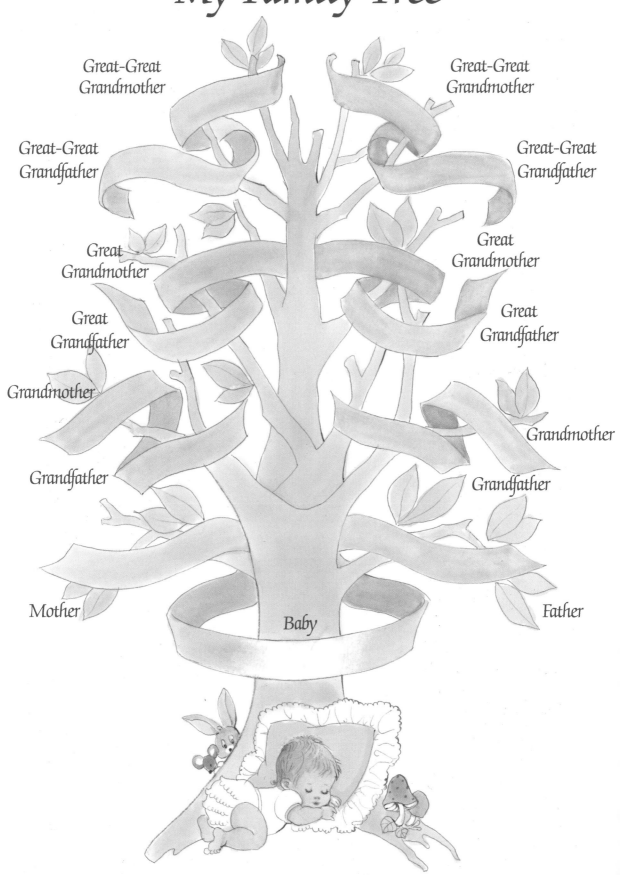

Great-Great
Grandmother

Great-Great
Grandmother

Great-Great
Grandfather

Great-Great
Grandfather

Great
Grandmother

Great
Grandmother

Great
Grandfather

Great
Grandfather

Grandmother

Grandmother

Grandfather

Grandfather

Mother

Baby

Father

My Relatives

Name	Relationship

I have baptized you in water; He will baptize you in the Holy Spirit.

Mark 1:8

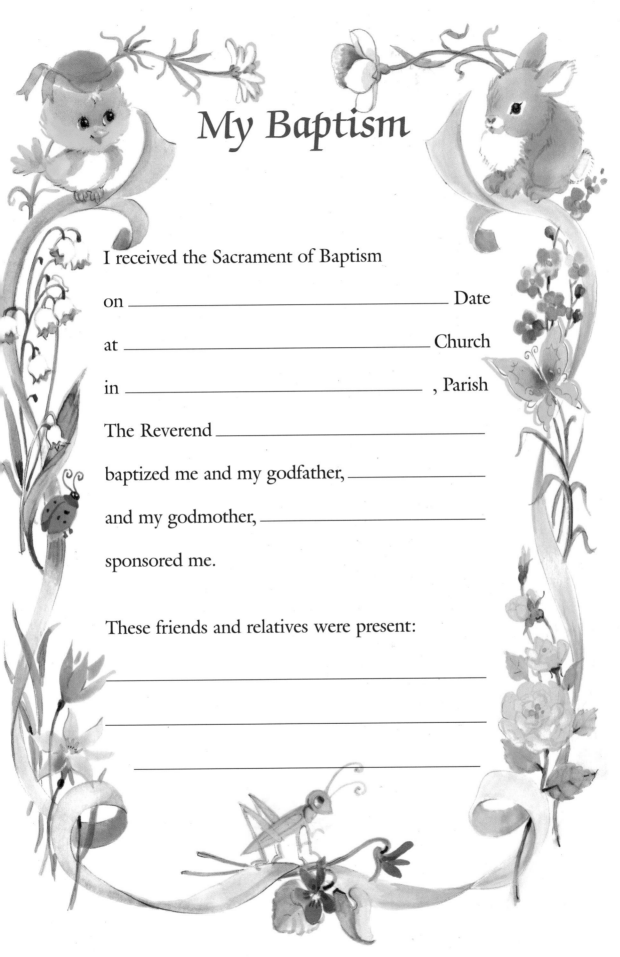

My Baptism

I received the Sacrament of Baptism

on _____ Date

at _____ Church

in _____ , Parish

The Reverend _____

baptized me and my godfather, _____

and my godmother, _____

sponsored me.

These friends and relatives were present:

_____

_____

_____

"O sing to the Lord a new song, for he has done marvelous things."

Psalm 98:1

My Early Development

MEMORABLE FIRSTS   Date

Held my head up _____

Turned my head _____

Had a bath _____

Recognized my mother _____

Recognized my father _____

Rolled over _____

Ate solid food _____

Recognized objects _____

Sat up _____

Crawled on all fours _____

Pulled myself up _____

Steps taken _____

Sounds uttered _____

Words spoken _____

Haircut _____

Tooth _____

Drew a picture _____

Began to count _____

Playmates _____

_____

OTHER FIRSTS _____

_____

_____

_____

"Make a joyful noise to the Lord, all the earth."

Psalm 100:1

My Favorite Things

Toys _____

_____

_____

Clothes _____

_____

Pets _____

_____

Games _____

_____

Stories _____

_____

Prayers _____

_____

Songs _____

_____

_____

T.V. Show _____

_____

_____

Playmates _____

_____

_____

Other Favorites _____

_____

_____

"Rejoice always, praying without ceasing,
Give thanks in all circumstances."

Ephesians 5:16

Other Memorable Firsts

My Mother and Father taught me how to pray as a child.
This is the first prayer I ever learned.

_____

_____

In time, I learned these important prayers.

_____ Age _____

_____ Age _____

_____ Age _____

On _____ at the age of _____
my Mother and Father brought me to_____
_____ Church
in _____

On_____ at the age of _____
I began my religious education at_____
_____ School
in_____
I was in _____ grade and my teacher was _____

I attended my first Mass on _____
at _____ Church
in _____
The Reverend_____was the celebrant.
I was _____ years old and these members of the family were present:

_____

_____

Other Sacraments
I Have Received

Reconciliation

I received the Sacrament of Reconciliation at the age of _____

on _____

at _____ Church

in _____ .

The Reverend _____ heard my confession.

Confirmation

I became a soldier of Christ on _____

at _____ Church

in _____ .

I was _____ years old.

Bishop _____ confirmed me

and _____ was my sponsor.

I took the name of _____ in Confirmation.

These members of my family were present: _____

_____

_____

_____

_____

_____

_____

First Holy Communion

I received Jesus in the Eucharist for the first time _____

on _____

at _____ Church

in _____ Parish.

I was _____ years old.

The Reverend _____ celebrated the Mass, and

The Reverend _____ gave me communion.

These members of my family were present: _____

_____

_____

_____

_____

_____

_____

_____

_____

_____

_____

*This day in David's city a savior has been born
to you, the Messiah and Lord.*

Luke 2:11

My First
Christmas

"For the love of Christ urges us on."

II Corinthians 5:14

My Travels
and Vacations

"We are God's children now, what we will be has not
been revealed."

I John 3:2

My First Birthday

Second Birthday

_____

_____

_____

_____

_____

_____

_____

Third Birthday

_____

_____

_____

_____

_____

_____

Fourth Birthday

_____

_____

_____

_____

_____

_____

_____

My Growth Chart

	Pounds and Ounces	Feet and Inches
Birth		
1 Month		
2 Months		
3 Months		
4 Months		
5 Months		
6 Months		
7 Months		
8 Months		
9 Months		
10 Months		
11 Months		
1 Year		
1½ Years		
2 Years		
2½ Years		
3 Years		
3½ Years		
4 Years		
5 Years		
6 Years		
7 Years		

"Bless the Lord, O my soul."
Psalm 103:22

My Dental Chart

Central Incisor, 7 ½ months

Lateral Incisor, 9 months

Cuspid, 18 months

First Molar, 14 months

Second Molar, 24 months

First Permanent Molar, 6 years

First Permanent Molar, 6 years

Second Molar, 20 months

First Molar, 12 months

Cuspid, 16 months

Lateral Incisor, 7 months

Central Incisor, 6 months

Visits to the Dentist

Date	Age	Doctor's Name

My Illnesses

Date	Age	Doctor's Name

My Medical Record

Immunizations	Date of Boosters	Series Completed	Doctor's Name
dpt { Diphtheria			
Tetanus			
Whooping Cough			
mmr { Measles			
Mumps			
Rubella			
Polio			
Other			

Tests	Date	Doctor's Name
Tuberculin		
Other		

Blood Type _____

Allergies	Doctor's Name	Remarks

"For I am the Lord who heals you."

Exodus 15:26

My Visits
to the Doctor

Date	Age	Remarks

"Happy are those who find wisdom, and those who get understanding... She is a tree of life to those."
Proverbs 3:13

My Schooling

Nursery School

_____
_____
_____
_____
_____
_____

Kindergarten

_____
_____
_____
_____
_____
_____

First Grade

_____

_____

_____

_____

_____

_____

Second Grade

_____

_____

_____

_____

_____

_____

Third Grade

_____

_____

_____

_____

_____

Fourth Grade

___

Fifth Grade

___

Sixth Grade

___

Photos